# Black Fathers
# &
# Strong Beginnings

# By Aaron Fields

Copyright © 2025 Aaron Fields. All rights reserved.

Published by The Write Perspective, LLC

**All rights reserved. No part of this book shall be reproduced or transmitted in any form or by any means, electronic, mechanical, magnetic, photographic including photocopying, recording or by any information storage and retrieval system, without prior written permission of the publisher. No copyright liability is assumed with respect to the use of the information contained in this book. Even though every precaution has been taken in preparation for this book, the publisher/author assumes no responsibility for errors or omissions. Neither is any liability assumed for any damage that results from the use of the information in this book.**

ISBN: 978-1-953962-68-3

🧠 **Food For Thought:**

**Showing up fully in the postpartum period to support the mother and nurture the newborn baby is imperative when it comes to strengthening families. For Black fathers, there is nothing wrong with learning, helping and healing.**

**The baby had finally arrived, and everything felt new. The days were slower, the nights were longer------but so much love filled in the air.**

The fathers knew the postpartum period was a sacred time. So, they learned -----about rest, bonding, babies, and healing.

**Some fathers became doulas. They learned how to massage tired shoulders, bring warm meals, and protect their women physically, emotionally, educationally, and spiritually.**

**Fathers made soups and smoothies to help mama's body recover from birth.**

**They listen when mama needed to cry, to laugh, or just sit in silence.**

**They did the dishes, folded the laundry, and kept things running------ so mama could rest.**

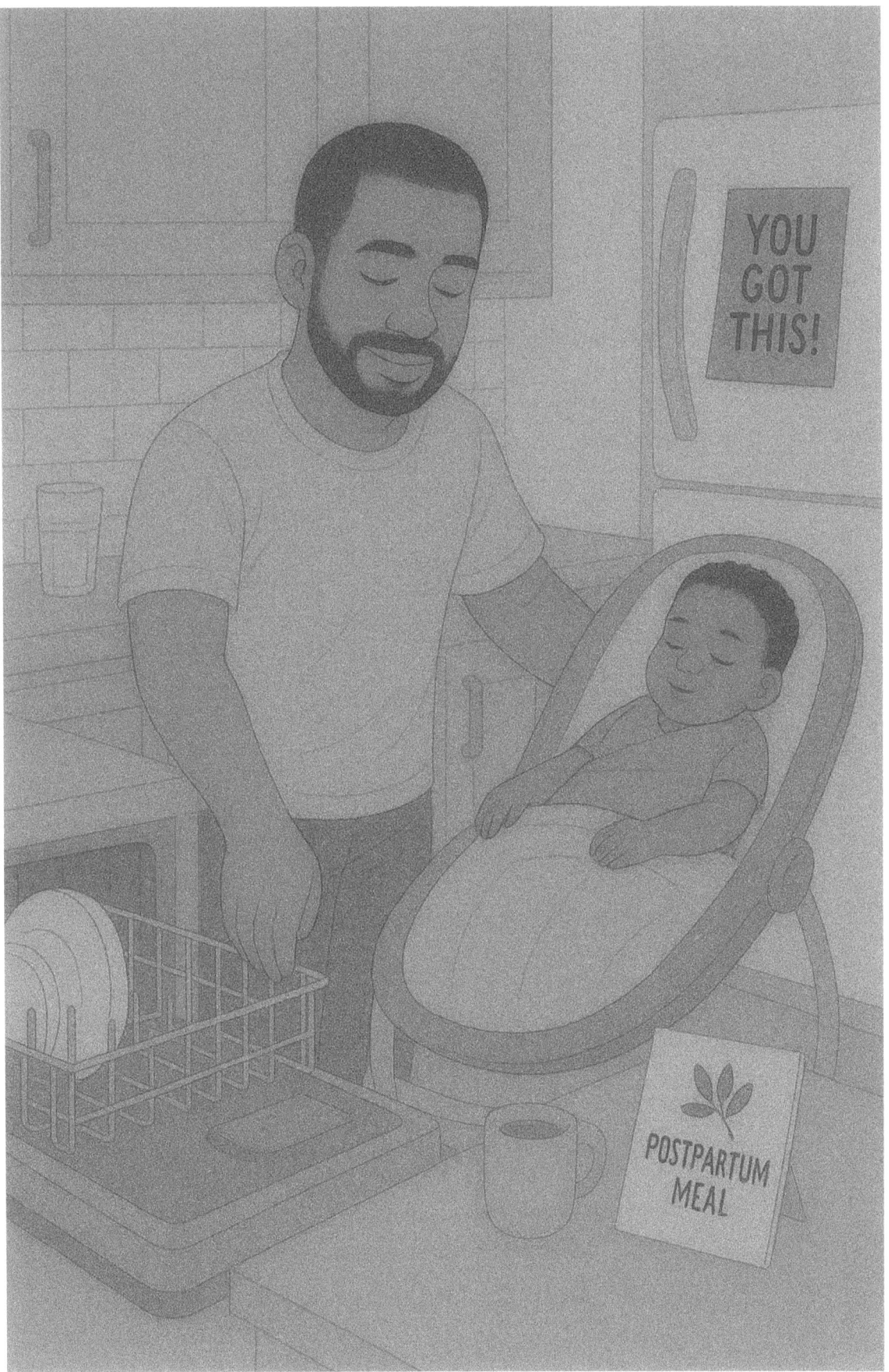

**Fathers held their babies close, heartbeat to heartbeat and skin-to-skin. That's how babies learn to feel safe.**

They changed diapers, gave tiny baths, and learned how magical a baby's smile can be.

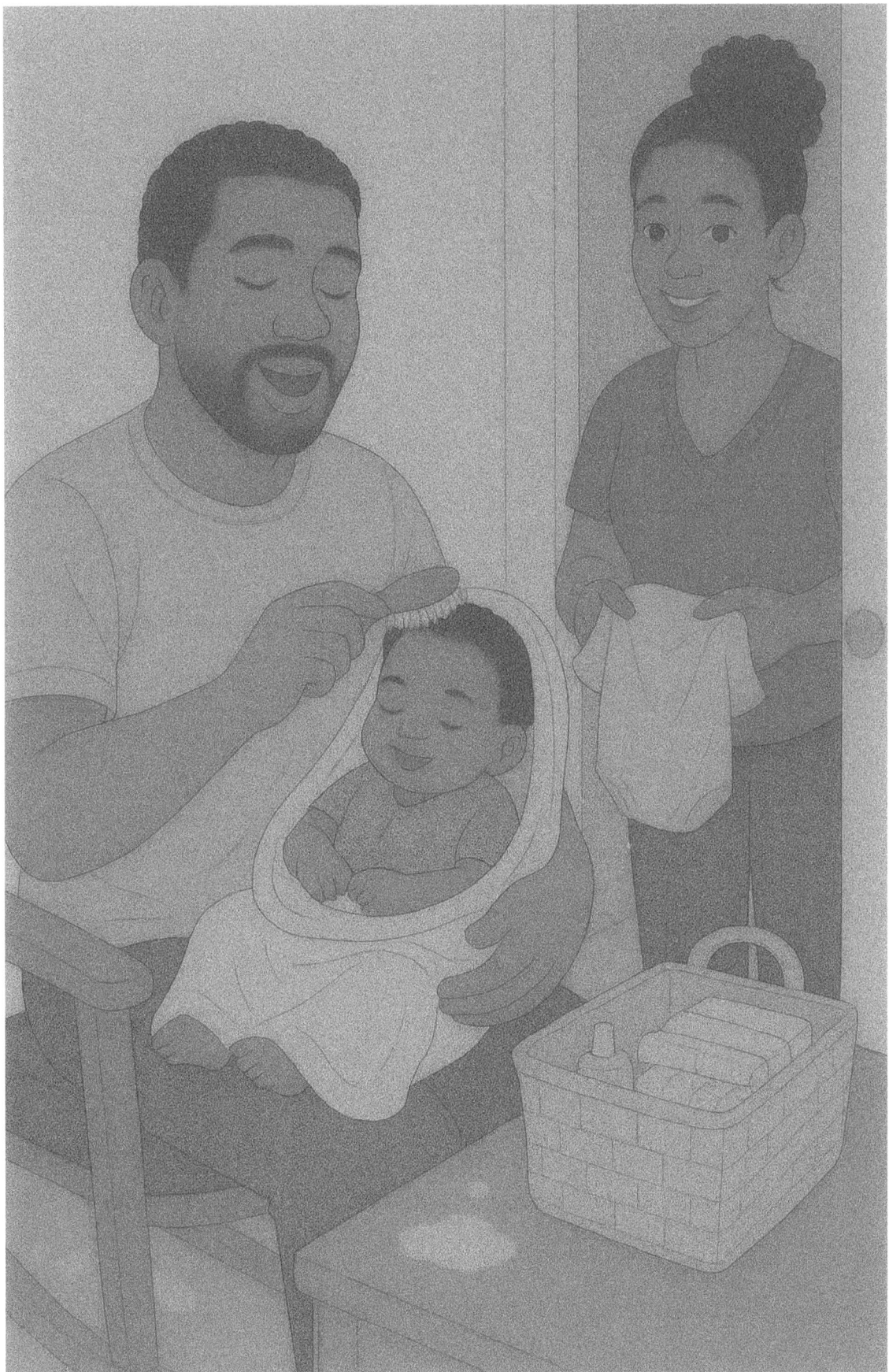

**They studied their baby's sounds, stretches, and sleepy cues------------like learning how to dance.**

**They reminded mama to drink water, take her herbs, and breathe. Healing takes time.**

"You're not alone." "You are loved." "We're doing this together". Their words held power.

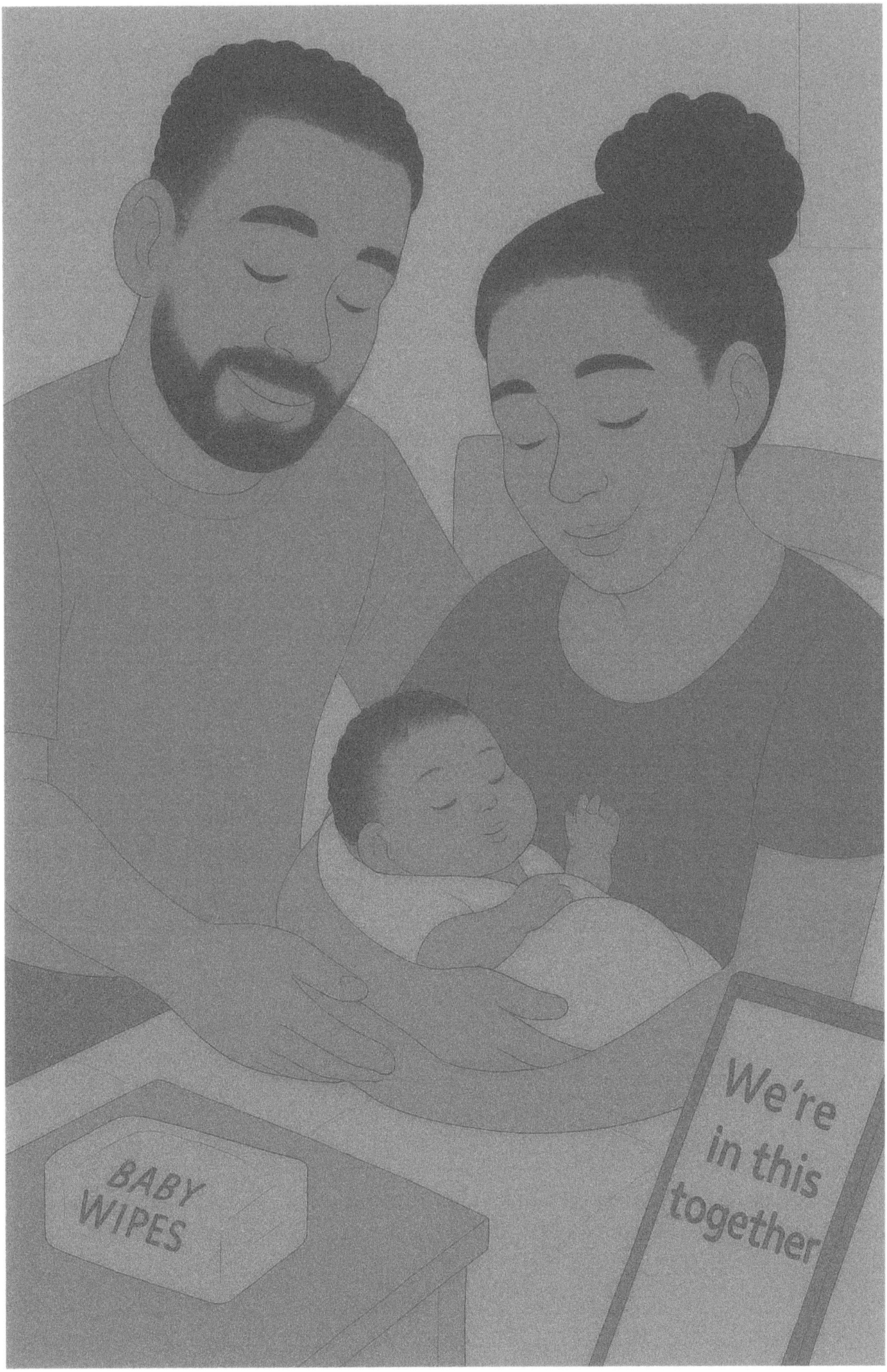
BABY WIPES
We're in this together

**When the baby napped, they all napped too. Rest is sacred.**

**Each day, they learned. Each day, they grew. As a family. As parents. As people.**

These fathers were building something new. A world where love leads, and everyone is cared for.

LOVE LEADS

**And in this beginning, the fathers stayed. The mothers healed. And the babies thrived.**

www.ingramcontent.com/pod-product-compliance
Lightning Source LLC
Chambersburg PA
CBHW041432040426
42450CB00021B/3472